Foodborne pathogens have no borders...so food safety is a must for all processors.

Allison Shearsett

Food Safety
For Food Processors
A Guide for Implementation

Allison Shearsett and Louis Bevoc

Published by
NutriNiche System LLC

Introduction

Most people do not expect to get sick or injured from the food they consume. After, it comes from food manufacturers who are regulated by the government, and those manufacturers operate under rules that protect the public from any type of risk. The problem with this thinking is the fact that it is only partially true. Yes, there are regulations in place for food manufacturers...but those regulations are sometimes bent, broken, misunderstood, or not enforced.

Unfortunately, millions of people are affected each year by some type of foodborne illness. They experience pain, hospital trips, and even death due to food related problems. The worst part about these illnesses is the fact that they could have been prevented if food safety measures had been implemented at the manufacturer, distributor, retailer, and consumer levels.

This book focuses on food safety for food manufacturers (also known as processors). First, it examines requirements imposed by government agencies, customers, and the processors themselves. Next, it looks at biological, chemical, and physical health hazards associated with processing. Then it looks at the impact of allergens on people and processes. Last, but certainly not least in the minds of food processing leaders, it explores food product recalls.

> *Note: Text that is bold-italicized shows examples that could be used in food processing plants. These examples are not complete, but they have real world application.*

Now that you understand the scope of this book, let's move into the ways that food safety controls are established at the manufacturing level. To do this, food safety requirements are discussed in the next section.

Requirements

Food processors have many rules in place for food safety. These rules regulate processes, procedures, and people in workplaces in order to make sure the products produced are safe for human consumption. These rules are established by:

Government agencies

Like they do for most other industries, the government oversees many different aspects of food processing. Regulations dictate what food processors can and cannot do, and most of those regulations are based on making sure the food produced is safe for people to eat.

The three major government overseers discussed in this book are the Food and Drug Administration (FDA), United States Department of Agriculture (USDA), and Center for Disease Control (CDC). Below is a description of the roles that these organizations play in regard to food safety.

Food and Drug Administration (FDA)

The FDA oversees the bulk of food manufactured in the United States. Their role is to protect the public by establishing and enforcing food safety rules and regulations. They form an alliance with state and local authorities to make the overall food safety system better and stronger.

The following is a general list of FDA responsibilities:

- Food (other than most egg, meat, and poultry)
- Food additives
- Beverages (water, milk, beer, soda, wine, etc.)
- Dietary supplements (vitamins, minerals, etc.)
- infant formulas

In its capacity, the FDA works to prevent food safety issues from occurring. They do this by requiring food processors to write food safety plans designed to identify food safety hazards that are likely to occur. Once those hazards are identified, controls need to be put in place to minimize them. These controls need to be monitored, and failures must be addressed with correction actions and preventative measures.

The following is an example of how a food safety hazard is addressed for a candy company:

Food safety hazard

Metal could get into the product during processing. This metal could come from broken equipment or machinery, and it could also come in with the raw materials (chocolate, sugar, honey, nuts, etc.)

Controls

Metal detection will be on every production line at the time of packaging for each box of product.

Monitoring of controls

Test wands made of ferrous, non-ferrous, and stainless steel will be put through the metal detectors every two hours to make sure they are working properly. If the metal detector does not detect the wands and shut down the line, then it is not working properly.

Corrective action

If a metal detector is found to not be functioning properly, then the line will be stopped until the problem is resolved and the unit is functioning correctly. Additionally, if the metal detector is found not to be working properly, all products back to the last acceptable check will be retained and run through the machine again once it is working properly.

The above example identifies the hazard as metal. It then incorporates metal detection as a control and monitors that control with test wands containing three common types of metal. If the metal detector fails to recognize any of these metals, then it is repaired and all products up to the last acceptable check are re-run through it.

Unfortunately, food safety plans do not always work as intended. If the plan is not effective, then the public gets contaminated or adulterated product. If news of this contamination reaches the FDA, then they will take action. Depending on the severity of the situation, the FDA can mandate a recall of the affected product (recalls are discussed in more detail later in this book).

The following is an example of how this happens using the candy company:

> A customer buys a box of caramel chocolate candy and breaks a tooth eating a piece. She knows she bit down on something hard and, upon examination, finds that it is a piece of hard plastic.

> The customer contacts the manager at the store where she bought the product. The manager contacts the FDA to report the incident, and the FDA sends an inspector to the candy plant to begin an investigation.

> With the inspector's help, the candy company discovers that piece of the plastic paddle used for mixing the caramel is missing. They look at their documentation and find that maintenance last recorded the paddles were in proper working order three weeks ago. They also know that caramel is used in three different types of chocolates.

> Based on the information the candy company has available, they initiate a recall for all three chocolate candies that contain caramel. The recall includes any product made over the last three weeks since that was the last documented check of the condition of the paddles.

> In this case, the candy company voluntarily conducted a recall. Their documentation supported the amount of product recalled, so the FDA did not need to mandate any action. They merely acted as an overseer of the recall process.

The FDA also has the authority to stop production at a food processor if they witness or have reason to believe that product has been intestinally adulterated. Food can be purposefully contaminated by competitors, disgruntled employees, or the general public for a variety of different reasons...and the FDA gets involved when this happens.

All processing records concerning food safety must be available to FDA inspection personnel upon request. They are authorized to make decisions based upon those records, and those decisions can be as severe as shutting down plants until product is considered safe for human consumption or corrective action is taken. Along the same lines, they can send products out for laboratory testing if processing records indicate they are adulterated in any way.

Contrary to what some people believe, the FDA also offers support to food processors. Inspectors understand government rules and regulations better than most people, and they can help managers of plants avoid pitfalls by offering simple advice. However, that advice must be limited because "consulting" by FDA inspectors is considered a conflict of interest that can jeopardize their Jobs.

United States Department of Agriculture (USDA)

The USDA oversees the bulk of meat, poultry, and egg products manufactured in the United States. They ensure that these products are safe, wholesome, and properly labeled following the same basic rules and regulations used by the FDA.

The USDA differs from the FDA for the following reasons:

- USDA issues establishment numbers for every processing facility and it is mandatory that these numbers be listed on every product along with the USDA mark of inspection (also known as an inspection legend). In general, FDA products do not require inspection legends or establishment numbers on finished products.
- USDA makes HACCP plans mandatory for all processing plants, and every product manufactured in those facilities must fall under those plans. This is not the case for all FDA processing plants.
- USDA has an everyday presence in the processing facilities that they regulate. The FDA is only present periodically or when needed due to food safety concerns.
- USDA requires approval of every product label from their labeling division. FDA does not require label approval.
- The USDA routinely samples products from every processing plant for pathogenic bacteria. Products from FDA processing plants are not routinely sampled.
- USDA and FDA have similar (and often times the same) rules in regard to food safety, but USDA plants are monitored more rigorously due to the fact the products being manufactured (meat, poultry, and eggs) are a higher risk for food safety.

Center for Disease Control (CDC)

The CDC provides a link between government agencies (FDA and USDA) and foodborne illnesses of consumers. They do this by tracking bacteria patterns (also known as DNA fingerprints) that identify outbreaks and pinpoint the sources of problems. The public can then be warned about avoiding these sources, and the government can begin procedures for containment and eradication.

The following is an example of the CDC in action:

A bacteria outbreak linked to milk sickens over 100 people in Michigan, Ohio, and Indiana. The CDC uses DNA fingerprinting to identify three rare strains of the E. coli that are closely related in terms of genetics.

This information leads investigators to look for a single source of the outbreak. They analyze milk samples from several different organizations and, by process of elimination, determine that source is a farm in Indiana.

CDC stops the farm from selling milk, and the public is warned about the E .coli problem associated with it. Dairy processors determine the products that utilized this milk, and a recall is put into effect.

The above example is similar to a real situation that occurred with cheese, and it shows how the CDC is able to attach foodborne illness to specific products and settings. They work to find, investigate, and control bacterial outbreaks before sickness spreads to large numbers of people.

External factors

The government plays a major role in making sure food processors produce safe products for people to eat. However, many other people are involved with food safety...and their roles are often just as important.

The following are examples of external factors that dictate food safety procedures for food processors:

Customer standards

Some customers have specific standards they want to be followed. For example, they might require that certain pieces of equipment are checked throughout the day for missing parts, or they require X-ray instead of metal detection. Many of these standards stem from problems customers have had in the past. They do not want these problems to reoccur, so they demand preventative food safety measures for the companies that manufacture their products.

Customer audits

Some customers conduct audits of the companies that manufacture their food products. These audits are performed by employees of the customers whose purpose is to make sure processors have food safety procedures in place.

Customer audits are commonly referred to as second-party audits. They are often based on written food safety agreements that have been established. Customers want to verify that processors are adhering to the specified requirements, so they conduct audits of those processors' facilities.

Third party audits

Third party audits are similar to customer audits except they are conducted by an independent third party. Typically these third parties are experienced auditors of food processing plants, and they target specific aspects of food safety.

Customers often request third party audits when they do not have the necessary in-house resources to conduct them or they want a non-bias professional review. Sometimes they want food processors to meet certain standards that can be verified by the third party. Other times they want food processors to achieve some type of certification that can be issued by the third party.

Internal programs

These programs are the heart of food safety. They are developed and implemented by the processors, and they are used by the government and auditors as support that food safety systems are in place and working as designed.

Important internal programs include:

Good Manufacturing Practices (GMP)

Food safety is arguably the most important aspect of food processing today. Every food plant management team must have some knowledge of the subject or they risk recall, temporary shutdown, and even loss of their business. This leads to a very good question. Where does the food processing owner or manager begin? The answer is Good Manufacturing Practices or GMPs. Without GMPs, food plants would certainly be at risk for sanitation and hygiene issues that lead to food safety problems.

GMPs are part of the foundation for a good food safety program. They help prevent food adulteration, food contamination (physical, chemical, and biological) and unsanitary processing conditions. A plethora of problems including wasted production time, shortened shelf life, spoilage, and recall can be avoided by adhering to GMPs. In other words, GMPs can keep a food plant out of a lot of trouble.

Planning is the key to developing good GMPs. When it comes to food safety, an ounce of prevention truly is worth a pound of cure. Plant management should implement specific policies so wholesome products can be manufactured. Written procedures should be distributed to employees, posted in conspicuous areas, and kept in an official file.

Training should be conducted to incorporate the GMP procedures and answer related questions. This training needs to be conducted in two parts:

Orientation

Employees should be trained before they start working. This prepares them for the jobs they are about to perform and eliminates the time and money issues involved with pulling employees off production lines. In short, management needs to meet with all new employees and review the organization's established GMPs to avoid the violation of those GMPs.

Annual

Employees should be trained on a yearly basis to implement updates, answer questions, and refresh memories. In addition to lectures, filming or videotaping employees doing their actual jobs can help accomplish this. Keep the footage brief...maybe 10 to 15 minutes. Point out when GMPs are being adhered to or violated using praise and constructive criticism. People tend to pay a great deal to a video or DVD that they personally appear in.

Many GMPs are listed in the United States Food and Drug Administration (FDA) regulations. These regulations address employees, plants, equipment, and processes for the manufacturing of many food products. They can be tailored to fit the specific needs of a wide variety of food processing plants.

This book cannot list good manufacturing practices for every type of food processor, but the following are some examples of simple GMPs that could be incorporated into a bakery:

1. Disease Control

    a. *Employees with open sores, infected wounds, or other microbial contamination will not work in production areas if contact with food or a food contact surface is reasonably likely to occur.*

    b. *Illnesses will be reported to plant management, and doctor's notes may be required before being allowed to return to work.*

2. Cleanliness and Personal Hygiene

    a. *Company supplied coats will be worn in all processing areas.*

    b. *Hands and/or gloves (of an impermeable material) will be washed and sanitized before entering production areas and anytime they become contaminated.*

    c. *Jewelry is not allowed, and rings will be covered by gloves.*

    d. *Hair nets will be worn by all personnel so that all hair is restrained, and beard nets will be worn when growth is exhibited.*

    e. *Personal items will not be stored in production areas.*

    f. *Eating, drinking, spitting, chewing gum, and smoking will not be allowed in production areas.*

3. Plant and Grounds

a. Equipment will be stored so grounds can be properly maintained.
b. Weeds adjacent to the building will be cut to discourage rodent harborage.
c. Grounds will drain to prevent pooling and potential breeding ground for pests.
d. Waste will be disposed of in a manner that discourages contamination.
e. Plant design and construction will facilitate sanitary operations and prevent pest infestation.
f. Lighting will be adequate for employees to perform the visual aspect of their job functions
g. Safety-type light bulbs and/or coverings will be used to prevent glass breakage.
h. Ventilation will be adequate enough so the growth of pathogenic organisms and pests are not promoted.

4. Sanitary Operations

a. Equipment will be disassembled, cleaned, and sanitized as needed to protect food against contamination.
b. Food contact surfaces and non-food contact surfaces will be cleaned and sanitized as needed to protect food against contamination.
c. Cleaning and sanitizing of equipment and food contact surfaces will follow instructions on container labels.
d. Pesticides, insecticides, and/or rodenticides will be applied by licensed professionals using caution to protect against food contamination.

5. Sanitary Facilities and Controls

a. All water will be potable (clean and suitable for drinking). This includes water used for processing, cleaning, and making ice.
b. Hot water (130F minimum) will be provided for washing hands and/or equipment.
c. Sewage and disposable waste will be properly conveyed from the facility.
d. Sanitary and properly maintained toilet facilities and welfare areas will be provided for all employees.
e. Signs directing employees to wash hands will be prominently displayed where appropriate
f. Trash receptacles will be designed to prevent harborage for pests and rodents, and those receptacles will not contact food.

6. Equipment and utensils

a. Equipment and utensils will be designed for easy cleaning

  b. *Equipment will be designed for protection against food contamination*

  c. *Equipment and utensils will be properly maintained*

  d. *Food contact surfaces will be corrosion resistant*

  e. *Instrumentation used to control critical parameters (pH, temperature, etc.,) will be calibrated and accurate.*

  f. *Coolers and freezers will be fitted with thermometers for temperature monitoring.*

7. Processes and Controls

  a. Raw materials and other food ingredients (liquid or dry) will be inspected at receiving and during production to ensure they are wholesome and suitable for processing. Specifically, employees will look for physical, biological, and chemical hazards. Letters of guarantee, along with chemical and microbiological specifications (meeting FDA standards for safe human consumption where applicable) will be available from all suppliers and may be requested if non-compliance is suspected.

  b. Packaging materials will be inspected at receiving and during productions to ensure they are in good condition. Letters of guarantee will be available from all suppliers and may be requested if conditions warrant the need.

    (1) Packaging materials will be received and stored in a manner designed to protect against physical, chemical, and biological contamination.

    (2) Packaging materials will be properly rotated using a First-in, first-out (FIFO) inventory method.

  g. *Processing will be conducted under conditions that minimize physical, chemical, and microbiological contamination.*

  h. *Food production areas and machinery will not be used for nonhuman food-grade products (pet food, animal feed, etc.).*

8. Warehousing and distribution

  a. *Storage and transportation of finished product will protect the food from physical, chemical, and biological contamination.*

  b. *Natural and/or unavoidable defects that present no health hazards will remain within FDA established limits.*

Now you understand the basic concept of GMPs, let's move into the next section that addresses sanitation in food plants...better known as SSOPs.

Sanitation Standard Operating Procedures (SSOP)

SSOPs differ from GMPs because the focus is on sanitation. GMPs should be taken into account when incorporating SSOPs into a processing plant's food safety program, but SSOPs detail sanitation tasks.

Essentially, SSOPs should address:

(1) The description of the task
(2) The purpose of the task
(3) The frequency of the task
(4) The individual(s) responsible for performing the task
(5) The procedure for performing the task (list all steps)
(6) The corrective action taken if the task is not properly completed

SSOPs are published in the Code of Federal Regulations. It states, "Each official establishment shall develop, implement, and maintain written standard operating procedures for sanitation (Sanitation SOP's)." Most meat and poultry plants refer to this section for implementation of SSOPs, but the general concept can be applied to all food processing plants.

First, the SSOP must be developed. Clear and concise procedures that prevent adulteration and contamination need to be written. Excessive wording often makes understanding and performing tasks more difficult. These procedures should list actions to be taken before and during processing on every day the plant operates.

An example of a pre-operational procedure is as follows:

A pre-operational inspection will be conducted by a designated employee every day before production start-up. Deficiencies and corrections will be noted on the pre-operational log, and food contact surface deficiencies will be discussed with the sanitation manager.

An example of an operational procedure is as follows:

Product will be removed from coolers under the direction of the sanitation supervisor before any cleaning of floors, walls, or ceilings begins. Any product coming in direct contact with cleaning chemicals will be condemned and put in inedible.

A responsible individual with the authority to make decisions for sanitation related issues should sign the SSOP upon implementation, anytime the program is modified, and once a year for reassessment. Her or his signature signifies that the establishment is adhering to the procedures outlined in the program.

An example of a change is the following:

On June 20, 2016, foaming sanitizers were removed from all finished product entrances. A dry quat known to kill Listeria will now be used.

*Signed:*_____   *Date:*_____

An example of a reassessment is the following:

> *On May 14, 2016, our SSOP program was reassessed and found to be acceptable.*
>
> *Signed:*_____   *Date:*_____

SSOPs should be continuously evaluated for effectiveness, even if the evaluations are not documented. Ineffective SSOPs often result in governmental intervention, which can make things much more difficult for everyone involved.

Prevention is the key to good SSOPs. Always remember to design SSOP plans that work and are feasible. Do not simply write something because it "looks good" on paper. Plants are held accountable for the plans they develop, so be sure that the personnel performing the tasks can follow everything that is written.

Corrective actions are also important. Corrective actions must (1) restore sanitary conditions, (2) ensure proper product disposition if necessary, and (3) prevent reoccurrence of the contamination or adulteration. Improvements or modifications to the existing SSOPs should also be detailed and documented.

Examples of sufficient and insufficient corrective action for a vegetable-slicing blade found to be improperly cleaned during preoperational inspection include:

Insufficient corrective action

> **The blade was cleaned.**

Sufficient corrective action:

> **The blade was removed, cleaned, and sanitized at 5:40 am. No product was involved. This problem will be discussed with our sanitation supervisor, and the responsible employee will be verbally reinstructed on proper cleaning of the slicer to avoid reoccurrence.**

Record keeping should be maintained in order to document the implementation and monitoring of SSOPs and corrective actions. Employees responsible for implementing and monitoring specific procedures should initial and date those procedures on a daily basis.

Records can be computerized or hand written. These records must be (1) maintained for a minimum of two years and (2) made available for government agencies' review within 24 hours of request.

FDA and USDA inspection personnel will verify an establishment's SSOP program periodically or when they feel it is necessary to verify effectiveness and adequacy. This verification includes:

    (1)   A general review of SSOP records
    (2)   An analysis of SSOP procedures and corrective actions
    (3)   Direct observation of the SSOP procedures specified
    (4)   Microbiological testing to access sanitary conditions

Keep in mind that supporting documentation is very important for establishing the effectiveness of an SSOP program...and history provides good supporting documentation. If a plant can show that established procedures have been successful over a period of time, then there will likely be less intervention by governmental inspection personnel.

Some essential components of SSOPs have been discussed. The following is an excerpt from a basic SSOP program that might be written for a dairy processing plant:

> *The sanitation manager will be responsible for implementing the SSOPs. Designated quality control employees will conduct pre-operational and operational inspection procedures. Any problems or deficiencies found will be documented, responsible employees will be notified, and corrective action will be administered.*
>
> *All soaps, sanitizers, and cleaners are stored in non-production areas, and they will be used per manufacturer recommendations and OSHA guidelines. All water used in the plant is potable. The term "washed" refers to the use of hot water only. The term "cleaned" refers to the use of hot water, soap, and sanitizer being used in the process. Sanitizers do not require rinsing.*
>
> *1. Raw Product Processing Areas*
>
> > *a. All machines will be disassembled (where possible) after each day's production. Residue will be removed by hand and put in inedible. Food contact surfaces will be cleaned (heavily soiled areas will be scrubbed with brushes). Nonfood contact Surfaces will be washed and/or cleaned*
> > *b. Utensils, knives, hand tools, lugs, and tables will be cleaned after each day's production.*
> > *c. Floors and walls will be cleaned after each day's production.*
> > *d. Drain baskets will be emptied in inedible containers and drains will be cleaned after each day's production.*
> > *e. Trash will be disposed of in designated, non-processing areas.*
> > *f. Condensation will be wiped when present and problems will be documented.*
> > *g. Problems resulting in potential contamination or adulteration of product will be immediately corrected or production will stop in the affected areas until the problem is corrected. All sanitation*

problems will be documented and discussed with sanitation personnel.

2. Finished Product Processing Areas

a. All machines will be disassembled (where possible) after each day's production. Residue will be removed by hand and put in inedible. Food Contact Surfaces will be cleaned (heavily soiled areas will be scrubbed with brushes). Non-food contact surfaces will be washed and/or cleaned

b. Utensils, knives, hand tools, lugs, and tables will be cleaned after each day's production.

c. Floors and walls will be cleaned after each day's production.

d. Drain baskets will be emptied in inedible containers and drains will be cleaned after each day's production.

e. Trash will be disposed of in designated, non-processing areas.

f. Maintenance personnel will wear designated color coats distinguishable from those worn by production employees when working on packaging machinery. Contact surfaces on machines will be sanitized after work is performed, if that work affects those surfaces.

g. When using hoses, care will be taken to assure that water is not splashed on any already cleaned and sanitized machines or equipment. Sanitized machines or equipment splashed with water will be re-cleaned and re-sanitized.

h. Condensation will be wiped when present and problems will be documented.

i. Problems resulting in potential contamination or adulteration of product will be immediately corrected or production will stop in the affected areas until the problem is corrected. All sanitation problems will be documented and discussed with sanitation personnel.

3. ADDITIONAL AREAS

a. Refrigeration Units

1. Unit pan will be cleaned
2. Coils and fins will be cleaned
3. Fan guards will be cleaned

b. Floors

1. Dry material will be swept and put in trash or inedible
2. Floors will be cleaned
3. Drains will be scrubbed and cleaned

c. Ceilings and Walls

1. *Residue or debris will be rinsed off*
2. *Ceilings and walls will be cleaned (and scrubbed if necessary)*

d. *Reoccurring problems will be discussed with responsible employees and management. Employees will be re-instructed in proper cleaning methodology if necessary.*

Now you have a general idea of what encompasses an SSOP program for a food processing plant. Next, let's move into HACCP...a program that was developed specifically for food safety.

HACCP (Hazard Analysis Critical Control Point)

HACCP refers to written programs that define procedures for food safety. They control biological, chemical, and physical hazards throughout processes in food manufacturing facilities. When effectively implemented, they prevent consumers from becoming ill or, in more serious cases, dying.

Food safety hazards are defined as follows:

Biological

This hazard results when disease-causing organisms enter food and pose a health threat to consumers. These organisms can be introduced at any time during processing, but they are often a result of poor handling, inadequate sanitation, or cross contamination.

The most common biological hazards are bacteria, but viruses and parasites also fall into this category. Each one of these is described below:

Bacteria

Pathogenic bacteria are the major enemy of food processors. They are responsible for a wide variety of food safety issues, and they often lead to production stoppages and recalls.

Some common bacteria that are associated with foodborne illness include:

- Bacillus cereus
- Campylobacter jejuni
- Clostridium botulinum
- Clostridium perfringens
- Escherichia coli 0157: H7

- Listeria monocytogenes
- Salmonella spp.
- Staphylococcus aureus

Viruses

Viruses insert themselves into host cells and alter the way those cells function. Unlike bacteria, viruses cannot survive without their living hosts. However, similar to bacteria, they can be very pathogenic and infectious.

Some common viruses that are associated with foodborne illness include:

- Bacteriophage
- Hepatitis A virus
- Norovirus
- Norwalk virus

Parasites

Similar to viruses, parasites grow in host organisms. However, unlike viruses, they do not supply their hosts with anything beneficial for survival...so their hosts tend to perish in relatively short periods of time.

Some common viruses that are associated with foodborne illness include:
- Cryptosporidium parvum
- Taenia spp.
- Toxoplasma gondii
- Trichinella spiralis
- Entamoeba coli

Chemical

This hazard results when chemicals enter food and pose a health threat to consumers. These chemicals can be introduced at any time during processing, but they are often a result of poor use or handling. Chemical contaminants can make people very sick, and that is why OSHA Safety Data Sheets (SDS) are required to list first aid procedures for ingestion.

Some common chemicals that are associated with foodborne illness include:

- Cleaning chemicals (soaps, sanitizers, cleaners)
- Maintenance chemicals (oil, gas, lubricants)

- The environment (air, water, earth)
- Food Additives (liquid, solid)
- Pesticides (sprays, liquids, pellets, blocks)

Physical

This hazard results when extraneous materials enter food and pose a health threat to consumers. These materials can be introduced at any time during processing, but they are often a result of poor handling or improper processing. Physical contaminants can cause choking, and they can damage people's mouths, teeth, and internal organs.

Some common chemicals that are associated with foodborne illness include:

- Cardboard
- Dirt
- Fingernails (fake or real)
- Glass
- Hair
- Metal
- Paper
- Plastic
- Stones
- Wood

The best way to describe a HACCP program is to define and exemplify the seven basic principles. These principles are as follows:

Principle 1: Perform a hazard analysis

Food processors need to determine the biological, chemical, and physical hazards that cause food to be unsafe and then identify preventive measures that will control those hazards. Every step in the process, from receiving to shipping, needs to be analyzed for food safety hazards. This analysis looks at the potential for each hazard to occur and determines if that potential is significant. If the potential is significant, then a measure for preventing it from occurring must be designated.

The example below shows three steps in the hazard analysis of a meat processing plant that manufactures ready-to-eat ham products:

FULLY COOKED, READY-TO-EAT
Ham

Ingredient/ Process Step	Potential hazard introduced, controlled or enhanced at this point	Is the potential food safety hazard significant?	Justification for decision	What control measures can be applied to prevent significant hazards?	Is this step a critical control point (CCP)?
SOAK CASINGS	B: Pathogens (Listeria, E. coli, Salmonella)	B: No	B: Low risk. Water is potable and contamination from soaking is unlikely.		B: No
	C: Contamination from cleaning agents or sanitizers	C: No	C: Low risk. GMP addresses storage of chemicals in non-processing areas, and all sanitizers are no rinse and follow container instructions.		C: No
	P: Foreign objects (metal, plastic, wood)	P: No	P: Low risk. Past history (one year) does not indicate contamination problems.		P: No
HANG ON RACKS	B: Pathogens (Listeria, E. coli, Salmonella)	B: No	B. Low risk. Products are stuffed in coolers below 40F. Cooler temperatures are monitored on GMP log		B: No
	C: Contamination from cleaning agents or sanitizers.	C: No	C: Low risk. GMP addresses storage of chemicals in non-processing areas, and all sanitizers are no rinse and follow container instructions.		C: No
	P: Foreign objects (metal, plastic, wood)	P: No	P: Low risk. Visually monitored by de-boning		P: No

			personnel, and past history (one year) does not indicate contamination problems.		
COOK	B: Pathogens (Listeria, Salmonella, and E. coli)	B: Yes	B: Finished Ham is considered ready-to-eat and Listeria, Salmonella, and E. coli could survive if lethality is not reached.	B: Proper finished internal temperature to reduce risk of pathogen survival.	B: Yes – CCP B1
	C: None identified (product is in an enclosed smokehouse with contact limited to the smokehouse person)	C: None identified	C: None required		C: No
	P: None identified (product is in an enclosed smokehouse with contact limited to the smokehouse person)	P: None identified	P: None required		P: No

In the above example, the first two processing steps (soak casings and hang on racks) do not present a biological, chemical, or physical hazard. However, the third step (cook) presents a biological hazard since Listeria, Salmonella, and E. coli (all three are pathogenic or disease causing bacteria) could survive if the proper temperature is not reached. Based on this potential, cooking is a critical control point (CCP). Critical control points are discussed in more detail in principle two.

Principle 2: Designate critical control points (CCPs)

Critical control points (CCPs) occur at steps in processing where controls can be used to prevent food safety hazards or reduce them to acceptable levels. For example, some foods need to reach a certain pH in order to be safe, while other foods need to be dried to a certain level (water activity) in order to be safe.

In the ham processing example, a critical control point occurs at the cook step. If the ham does not reach a certain temperature, then there is a reasonable risk that it might be safe to eat due to Listeria, Salmonella, and E.

coli. Cooking can eliminate these pathogens and reduce the risk to an acceptable level.

Principle 3: Establish critical limits

Critical limits for the CCP need to be established. In other words, maximum and/or minimum values must be implemented so the CCP is effective in eliminating the risk or reducing it to an acceptable level.

In the ham processing example, the critical limit implement involves temperature. Specifically, all ham must be cooked to 160F minimum internal temperature. Listeria, Salmonella, and E. coli cannot survive at 160F, so the risk is reduced to an acceptable level.

Principle 4: Establish monitoring requirements

Monitoring requirements of the CCP need to be established. Monitoring is the actual performing of the CCP that keeps the designated food safety hazard(s) from occurring.

In the ham processing example, a designated employee uses a calibrated temperature to establish that the internal temperature of the visibly largest ham on each rack of product is at least 160F.

Principle 5: Establish corrective actions

Corrective actions describe the action that will be taken when monitoring activities exceed established critical limits. This action ensures that contaminated or adulterated product does not reach consumers.

In the ham processing example, all parts of 417.3 (corrective action) in Directive 5000.1 will be addressed. Specifically, this states:

   (1) The cause of the deviation is identified and eliminated
   (2) The CCP will be under control after the corrective action is taken
   (3) Measures to prevent recurrence are established
   (4) No product that is injurious to health or otherwise adulterated as a result of the deviation enters commerce.

Principle 6: Establish record keeping requirements

Records that are important to the HACCP plan need to be documented and maintained. These records pertain to the CCP, and they are used as support for the HACCP program. Deviations and corrective actions should also be listed on these records.

In the ham processing example, cooking logs and thermometer calibration logs are the records that need to be documented and maintained. Cooking logs record the finished temperatures of the ham and thermometer calibration logs indicate the thermometers used to take the temperatures are accurate.

Principle 7: Establish verification and validation

This principle has two parts. The first part is verification, and the second part is validation. Both of these are ongoing processes, but verification is done more frequently than validation. Verification is also documented in the HACCP program, while this is not typically the case for validation.

The following is a description of both parts:

Verification

Verification entails observing the monitoring activities and reviewing the records. This confirms that the monitoring activities are following those specified in the HACCP plan, and it assures the records are accurate.

In the ham processing example, quality control personnel verify the monitoring activities weekly to assure they are meeting those specified. Specifically, they watch the monitoring employee to assure the minimum internal temperature reached is 160F and the largest piece of ham on every rack has the temperature taken. The cooking logs and thermometer calibration logs are also reviewed weekly to assure that they are accurate and complete.

Validation

Validation ensures that the HACCP plan is doing what it is designed to do. In other words, is it working properly to prevent the food safety hazard(s) from occurring? The type of action taken and the frequency of that action need to be documented.

In the ham processing example, validation is accomplished by sending finished product out to a lab for microbial analysis on a yearly basis. This is written as follows:

> *Once a year a ham will be sent to an accredited laboratory and analyzed for Listeria, Salmonella, and E. coli. Negative results indicate the plan is working, and positive results will require a plan reassessment.*

Below is the HACCP plan for the ham processing example. The table lists every principle discussed above.

Product Category	Process Step	CCP	CCP Description	Critical Limits	Monitoring	Corrective Action	HACCP Records	HACCP System Verification
Ham	Cook	CCP B1	Survival of pathogens (Listeria, Salmonella and E. coli)	Internal meet a minimum of 160F	Monitoring employee takes the internal temperature of the visibly largest piece of ham on every rack using a calibrated hand held thermometer.	Quality Control will address all parts of 417.3 (corrective action) in Directive 5000.1.	Cooking logs and thermometer calibration logs are on file.	Monitoring activities are observed once per week. Quality control employee initials indicate monitoring procedures are acceptable as outlined in the HACCP plan. Records (cooking logs and thermometer calibration logs) are reviewed once per week. Quality control employee initials indicate records are complete and accurate.

Now you understand the basic of a food safety HACCP plan. This leads us to food security...another program essential for assuring unsafe product does not reach consumers.

Food security

Food security programs protect food from tampering, contamination, or other forms of adulteration. They do this by preventing unauthorized personnel from gaining access to food or water supplies and by providing plans for emergency situations. In short, they list current controls in place, and outline strategies for catastrophes.

The following is an excerpt from a basic food security program that might be written for a frozen dinner processing plant:

1. *Controls currently in place include:*

A. *Employee only entrance – Production employees must enter the building through one door, and visitors are not allowed to enter the building through this door. Any visitor seen at this entrance throws up a red flag and questions are asked as to why this person is at our establishment.*
B. *Sign-in sheet at visitor's entrance – all visitors must sign in and identify their company and the person they want to meet with.*
C. *Alarmed points throughout the plant – The alarm system has many checkpoints that monitor the facility when employees are not in the building.*
D. *Fenced premises– fenced areas are locked and a guard allows access.*
E. *Cameras with monitors at all entrances – plant entrances (and some processing areas) are continually monitored.*
F. *Limited roof access – only one door leads to the roof.*
G. *Exterior lighting - lights the entire building.*
H. *Backflow devices are on all processing water outlets.*
I. *Trucks are examined by receiving personnel for defects and foreign material.*
J. *All raw materials are inspected at the receiving dock.*
K. *Product coolers are locked when production ends.*
L. *Designated people have keys and lock doors after production.*
M. *Product inventories are monitored and recorded by designated personnel.*

2. *Potential Contamination and Action Taken*

A. *Power Failure*

1. *Communication via cell phones.*
2. *Provide management personnel with flashlights*
3. *Determine if the building should be evacuated*
4. *Check for trapped people in all areas (processing areas, elevators, stairways, etc.)*
5. *Call emergency contacts as determined necessary (refrigeration contractor, electrician, electric and gas company, etc.)*
6. *Conduct an onsite inspection to determine if the problem is in our location only, and if not, try to find out when power will be restored*
7. *Shut down all equipment that could be damaged when power is restored*
8. *Cover exposed product and keep all refrigerator and freezer doors closed*
9. *Document all injuries/incidents/expenses incurred*

B. *Severe Weather/Tornado*

1. *Provide flashlights to management personnel*
2. *Monitor the weather through some channel of communication (radio, television, internet, etc.)*
3. *Locate safe areas of the building (areas away from glass and windows) for harborage if necessary.*
4. *Announce status or updates over the page system if necessary*
5. *Cover exposed product and keep all refrigerator and freezer doors closed*
6. *Keep in constant communication via cell phones*
7. *Document all injuries/incidents/expenses incurred*

C. *Water Contamination*

1. *Stop all production and cleaning where water is used*
2. *Locate all product exposed to the contaminated water and retain pending laboratory analysis*
3. *Used bottled water (or boiled water if possible) for any processing or consumption.*
4. *After the problem is resolved, flush all lines for 10 minutes and then rinse, wash, and sanitize all food contact surfaces.*
5. *Document all findings*

D. *Product Contamination*

1. *Stop production in the affected area*
2. *Refer to the HACCP plan for determining if the contamination specifics (chemical, physical, or biological hazard)*
3. *Identify potential witnesses*
4. *Consider product laboratory analysis*
5. *Issue a product recall if necessary*
6. *Document all findings*

Pest control

Pest control programs are implemented to stop pests from entering food processing facilities (rats, mice, birds, etc.) or kill pests once they have entered the building (flies, mosquitoes, roaches, etc.). The major two major categories of these programs are rodent control and pest control.

The following is a description of both categories:

Rodent control

These are the most notorious pests threatening the food supply. Rodents cause a lot of damage in food processing plants, and they are easily capable of spreading disease. Once in a plant, they can multiply rapidly and create a situation that is very difficult to resolve.

Rodent evidence comes in the form of droppings, urine trails, footprints, damaged food, and gnawed containers. They can live just about anywhere there is harborage, and have been known to burrow in walls or underground. In general, they are survivalists...and they present a daunting challenge in terms of eradication.

Food processors need to rodent-proof their facilities. This is done by sealing all openings/gaps and eliminating harborage, such as unused equipment and machinery, inside and outside of plants. Indoor traps and outdoor poison bait stations are also used as defense mechanisms. If rodents do enter the building, they need to be immediately destroyed to prevent food adulteration.

Insects

These pests might not be as notorious in food plants as rodents, but they are more common. Insects include flies, mosquitoes, cockroaches, and spiders...and they are capable of transmitting disease and contaminating food products.

Insects can be found dead or alive in food...with some even using the food as their homes. They mostly live in non-refrigerated environments, and most prefer processing areas that are slightly warmer than normal room temperature. They typically do not pose the same level of threat as rodents, but they can be difficult to eliminate once they enter processing areas.

Food processors need to insect-proof their facilities. This is done by sealing all openings/gaps and eliminating harborage, such as pooling water, inside and outside of plants. Glue boards and insect-o-cuters are also used as defense mechanisms. If insects do enter the building, they need to controlled or destroyed to prevent food adulteration.

The following is an excerpt from a basic pest control program that might be written for a pasta processing plant:

A. *Housekeeping: All processing areas and equipment will be cleaned daily if used or whenever necessary. All storage areas will be kept clean and uncluttered.*
B. *Structural: All drains will be equipped with screens and/or covers. All potential rodent entrance points, such as cracks and holes, will be repaired immediately.*
C. *Exterior: The premises will be kept clean and uncluttered. lawn, weeds, and brush will be kept trimmed. All areas of harborage will be eliminated.*
D. *A current list of all pesticides in use will be maintained. All pesticides will be EPA approved.*

E. *Rodenticides: Rodenticides will be placed in bait boxes at designated areas outside the building. The rodenticide bait will be a distinctive blue-green color for identification purposes. Bait boxes will be checked monthly and recorded on the Rodent Control Service Record.*

F. *Rodent Stations: Rodent stations will be placed at designated areas every 30 feet inside the non-production areas of the building. Rodent stations will be checked weekly and recorded on the In-House Rodent Control Service Record.*

G. *Electronic Insect Control: Electronic "Insect-A-Cutors" are placed strategically throughout the plant in non-production areas. The catch pans are large enough to ensure that dead insects will not fall to the floor. The pans will be cleaned bi-monthly, or sooner if necessary, during periods of use.*

H. *Sticky Board Insect Control: Sticky board insect control traps will be placed in production areas. These are changed as needed based on the insect populations seen on the boards.*

I. *Detection of Rodent Evidence: If rodents or evidence of rodents is detected in the plant the following action will be taken:*

1. *Operations are immediately stopped in the affected area.*
2. *All packaging materials and containers are examined for rodent damage and discarded if contaminated.*
4. *Product showing evidence of rodent contamination is condemned, placed in inedible containers and denatured.*
5. *All harborage is removed from the area.*
6. *The entire area and equipment are completely washed and sanitized.*
7. *A complete survey of the plant and premises is taken to ensure that all points of entry and areas of harborage are eliminated.*
8. *Production will resume after plant personnel are satisfied that the problem is corrected and the area is cleaned.*

Now that you understand many of the internal and external food safety requirements imposed on food processors, let's move into a discussion on a topic that has gained a lot of attention in regard to food safety. That topic is allergens.

Allergens

Food allergies occur when people's immune systems have abnormal responses to food. Sensitivity to allergens varies from person to person, but worst case sceneries result in death.

For food safety reasons, food processors should have written programs in place that address the allergens they are using in their products. These programs help make certain that allergens are properly listed on ingredient statements and monitored for misuse and cross-contamination.

The major eight food allergens are soy, wheat, milk, eggs, fish, shellfish, peanuts, and tree nuts. These allergens are described below.

Soy

This is likely the most common allergy. The symptoms of soy reactions are usually mild, but certain cases are more severe. FDA law dictates that soy must be listed in ingredient statements if it is used in food products. However, some processors fail to adhere to this law, and that failure can result in allergic reactions and recalls.

Food or food ingredients containing soy include:

- Miso
- Soya
- Soybean
- Soy fiber
- Soy flour
- Soy milk
- Soy protein
- Soy sauce
- Tempeh
- Textured vegetable protein
- Tofu

Wheat

The bad news about wheat allergies is that they are most common in children. The good news about wheat allergens is that children usually outgrow them before they become adults.

The symptoms of wheat reactions range from mild to severe, and FDA law dictates wheat must be listed on ingredient statements of products containing it. However, some products, such as dextrose made from wheat, do not list wheat...so food processors are not aware that it is present.

Wheat allergies should not be confused with the gluten intolerance associated with individuals suffering from Celiac Disease. Gluten is a combination of proteins found in wheat, rye, oats, barley, spelt, and other similar grains. Wheat allergies typically cause hives, itching, and breathing difficulties, while gluten intolerance results in more severe problems including permanent damage of intestines.

Food or food ingredients containing wheat include:

- Breadcrumbs
- Bulgur
- Cereal extract
- Couscous
- Cracker meal
- Durum
- Einkorn

- Emmer
- Farina
- Flour (various types)
- Hydrolyzed wheat protein
- Matzah
- Pasta
- Seitan
- Semolina
- Spelt
- Triticale
- Wheat bran
- Wheat durum
- Wheat germ
- Wheat gluten
- Wheat grass
- Wheat malt
- Wheat protein
- Wheat starch

Milk

Similar to wheat allergies, milk allergies are also more common in children who outgrow them later in life. Symptoms range from mild to severe, and FDA law dictates milk must be listed on ingredient statements of products containing it.

Milk allergies should not be confused with lactose intolerance. Lactose intolerant individuals lack the enzyme necessary to digest the sugar lactose. The inability to digest lactose results in extreme intestinal discomfort...unlike the typical hives and itching that result from milk allergies.

Food or food ingredients containing milk include:

- Butter
- Buttermilk
- Candy
- Caramel
- Casein
- Cheese
- Chocolate
- Cottage cheese
- Cream
- Custard
- Evaporated milk
- Ghee
- Half-and-half
- Milk (all types)
- Milk powder
- Milk protein

- Pudding
- Sour cream
- Whey (all forms)
- Whey protein hydrolysate
- Yogurt

Egg

Similar to milk and wheat, egg allergies are also common in children. The whites contain the harmful allergenic proteins, but individuals with allergies need to avoid consuming any part of the egg. Symptoms range from mild to severe, and FDA law dictates egg must be listed on ingredient statements of products containing it.

Food or food ingredients containing egg include:

- Albumen
- Dried egg
- Eggnog
- Egg white
- Egg yolk
- Lysozyme
- Mayonnaise
- Meringue
- Powdered egg
- Ovalbumin
- Surimi

Fish

Fish allergies affect people of all ages, and many individuals do not outgrow them. Symptoms can be very severe, and FDA law dictates fish must be listed on ingredient statements of products containing it.

Food or food ingredients containing fish include:

- Anchovies
- Bass
- Catfish
- Cod
- Flounder
- Grouper
- Haddock
- Hake
- Halibut
- Herring
- Perch
- Pike

- Pollock
- Salmon
- Swordfish
- Sole
- Trout
- Tuna

Shellfish

Fish allergies affect people of all ages, and many individuals do not outgrow them. In fact, some people do not experience their first allergic reaction until well into adulthood. Symptoms can be very severe, and FDA law dictates shellfish must be listed on ingredient statements of products containing it.

Food or food ingredients containing shellfish include:

- Barnacle
- Clams
- Crab
- Crayfish
- Krill
- Lobster
- Mussels
- Oysters
- Prawns
- Scallops
- Scampi
- Shrimp

Peanut

Peanut allergies are fairly common in people of all ages. However, symptoms stand out from other allergies because they can be fatal. Simply touching products containing peanuts can trigger allergic reactions, and people die every year from peanut ingestion. FDA law dictates peanuts must be listed on ingredient statements of products containing them.

Peanuts should not be confused with tree nuts. Peanuts are part of the legume family and grow underground, while tree nuts are true nuts and grow on trees.

Food or food ingredients where peanuts are commonly found include:

- Bread
- Cake
- Candy
- Chocolate
- Coffee Cake
- Croissants

- Donuts
- Fudge
- Ice cream
- Peanuts
- Peanut brittle
- Peanut butter
- Rolls
- Salads

Tree nut

Tree nut allergies occur in adults and children, and people usually do not outgrow them. Symptoms can be severe...even resulting in death in some rare situations.

As noted earlier, tree nuts grow on trees, and they are part of the nut family. They are not part of the legume family that includes peanuts.

Food or food ingredients where tree nuts are commonly found include:

- Almond
- Beechnut
- Brazil nut
- Bread
- Butternut
- Cake
- Candy
- Cashew
- Chestnut
- Chocolate
- Coffee Cake
- Croissants
- Donuts
- Filbert
- Fudge
- Hickory nut
- Ice cream
- Macadamia nut
- Nut butters (cashew butter, pecan butter)
- Nut meal
- Nut milk (cashew milk, almond milk)
- Nut paste (filbert paste, almond paste)
- Pecan
- Pili nut
- Pine nut
- Pistachio
- Praline
- Rolls

- Salads
- Shea nut
- Walnut

People are also allergic to other foods, but these allergies are not quite as common as the eight listed above. These other foods include:

Sesame

Sesame allergies occur in people of all ages, and the number of individuals experiencing effects appears to be increasing. Symptoms can be mild to severe, depending on the sensitivity of the person.

Food or food ingredients where sesame is commonly found include:

- Benne
- Bread
- Coffee cake
- Halvah
- Sesame flour
- Sesame oil
- Sesame paste
- Sesame salt
- Sesame seed
- Sesemolina
- Sim
- Tahini
- Turkish cake

Mustard

Mustard allegories are less common than other allergies, but they are a problem for some people. Canada considers mustard a major allergen, but the United States does not. Symptoms can be mild to severe depending on sensitivity.

Food or food ingredients where mustard is commonly found include:

- Barbeque Sauce
- Curry
- Mayonnaise
- Mustard
- Mustard oil
- Mustard seed
- Pickles
- Pizza
- Processed meats

- Salads
- Salad dressings

Other

Some people also experience allergic reactions to corn and meat. Since corn is used in many different foods, this can be a problem. Along the same lines, meat is a "center of the plate" item that is consumed on a daily basis by many people...so it can also present issues.

Sulfites are the last item that needs to be mentioned in this section. They present a sensitivity issue for some people, and allergen type symptoms can result.

Food or food ingredients where sulfites are commonly found include:

- Bakery items
- Beer
- Candy
- Canned vegetables
- Cider
- Condiments
- Dried fruit
- Gravy
- Jellies and jams
- Lemmon Juice
- Maraschino cherries
- Molasses
- Pickled food
- Potassium bisulfite
- Sulfite
- Sulfur dioxide
- Vegetable juice
- Wine

Allergen program

The following is an example of a basic allergen program that might be written for a specialty croissant processing plant:

A. **Allergens consist of the following:**

Milk, soy, fish, peanuts, tree nuts (e.g., almonds, pecans, walnuts), shellfish, eggs, wheat, mustard, sesame, and sulfites

The following allergens may be used in our products:

Soy protein, wheat flour, milk, egg yolks, peanut oil

B. *Pallets of ingredients are identified with the specific allergen upon being received.*

C. *Allergens are stored in designated areas and identified.*

D. *Copies of formulas for all items are on file electronically.*

E. *Scaled ingredients list applicable allergens.*

F. *Ingredient labels follow products throughout processing (work in process) to ensure that allergens are listed on every rack of product.*

G. *Purchasing has informed all ingredient suppliers that ingredient statements cannot be changed without prior notice.*

H. *Color-coded or labeled scoops are used for allergens and other ingredients with potential to cause adverse reactions as follows:*

   - *Blue – Soy*
   - *Marked Blue – Wheat*
   - *Green – Milk*
   - *White – Egg*
   - *Clear - Peanuts*

I. *Spillage - in the event of allergen spillage the following will be done:*

   - *Solid Allergen Spillage*

   Details will be recorded in the Allergen Spillage Log. The situation will be risk assessed for potential cross-contamination, and any cross-contaminated product will be put in the trash. The area will be cleaned with dedicated cleaning equipment and damaged product will be put in the trash.

   - *Liquid Allergen Spillage*

   Details will be recorded in the Allergen Spillage Log. The situation will be risk assessed for potential cross-contamination, and any cross-contaminated product will be put in the trash. Paper towels will be used to remove the product and put in the trash. The floor will then be washed.

J. *Products containing allergens are physically separated by racks that do not allow cross contamination.*

K. *Product flow from receiving to shipping is one way to minimize cross contamination.*

L. *For traceability purposes, ingredient codes used in each batch of product are logged on a checklist.*

M. *Production lines are cleaned (using wipes or sanitizer) between unlike products. All processing areas are cleaned daily after production is finished.*

N. *Employees change aprons, sleeves, and gloves when moving from one line to another or working on products containing different allergens.*

O. *All finished products meet FDA labeling specifications.*

P. *For traceability and identification purposes, all finished product are coded with a "sell by," "pack date," "use or freeze by," lot number, and/or Julian code.*

Q. *Allergen testing will be conducted quarterly to verify the program is working. Testing consists of swabbing a food contact line after a product with a known allergen has passed over that line and the line has been cleaned in preparation for the next product. If results show greater than 5 ppm of the known allergen, then the allergen program needs to be re-assessed.*

Now you understand the relationship between allergens and food safety. Next, let's look at the action taken when products with food safety concerns inadvertently reach the public. This action is commonly known as a recall.

Recalls

Recalls occur when food products available to the public pose some type of health risk. This risk can occur for a variety of different reasons, but the most common factors are listed below.

Health hazards

This refers to recalls that result from biological, chemical, or physical hazards reaching the public. An example is as follows:

The Stanford Salad Company processes pasta salad that they sell to delicatessens. A deli manager receives a complaint from two different customers that they became ill after eating some of Sanford's product. Both customers ate pasta salad with a lot number of 6315. This is alarming to the deli manager, and he pulls the product from hi counter. He promptly notifies Sanford that lot 6315 pasta salad has a problem.

Sanford obtains some of lot 6315 pasta and sends it out to a laboratory for microbial analysis. They find that it is contaminated with Listeria monocytogenes...a potentially deadly bacterium. They also analyze other lots of the same product and find that they are not contaminated with any pathogens.

Based on their findings, Sanford recalls all pasta with a lot number of 6315. This is an entire day of production, and it results in over 2000 pounds of pasta salad being recalled.

This recall resulted from a biological hazard, Listeria monocytogenes, which was in the product when it reached consumers.

Allergens

This refers to recalls that result from products containing allergens that are not listed on the ingredient statements. An example is as follows:

The Holland Bros. Bakery manufactures bread and rolls for hotel chains. They make a sweet roll that contains pecans for hotel brunches, and this product is distributed all over the city of Chicago.

A hotel guest becomes ill after eating one of Holland Bros. sweet rolls. She breaks out with hives and has difficulty breathing. She knows she can eat pecans....but she is allegoric to peanuts. She informs the hotel manager, and the manager calls Robert Holland, president of Holland Bros. Bakery, to tell him what happened.

Robert checks his production records and finds that his employees mixed peanuts in the affected batch of sweet rolls instead of pecans. Robert promptly begins to recall this lot of sweet rolls. Fortunately, all of this lot (22 dozen rolls) went to the same hotel chain, so he is able to get it back to his facility by making a few phone calls.

This recall resulted from an allergen, peanuts, which were in the product when it reached consumers.

Lack of inspection

This is the most interesting reason for a recall, and it is likely the least understood by the general public. USDA processing plants can only produce meat and poultry products when USDA inspectors are on the job. If they process product during hours that USDA inspectors are not working, the product made during that time is subject to a recall if leaves the control of the processing establishment.

Selander Meat International (SMI) produces fresh sausage products for restaurants. They normally work Monday through Friday to complete orders, but they have a machine breakdown and need to produce sausage on Saturday.

SMI schedules production on Saturday, but they forget to let the USDA inspector know that they are working. A week later, the USDA inspector is reviewing records and notices the Saturday production. He asks where this product is located and is told that it has been shipped.

The USDA inspector calls his boss, and she mandates a recall because SMI operated without "the benefit of inspection." They have to contact three different distributors, who get the word out to the restaurants that have purchased the product. Over 8000 pounds of sausage is recalled.

This recall resulted from a lack of inspection in a USDA regulated facility.

Recall program

The following is an excerpt of a basic recall program that might be written for an ice cream processor:

A. **RECALL CLASSIFICATIONS**

    1. *Class I. A situation where there is a reasonable probability that use of the product will cause a serious health hazard including death.*
    2. *Class II. A situation where there is a remote possibility of adverse health consequences from use of the product.*
    3. *Class III. A situation where use of the product is very unlikely to cause adverse health consequences.*

B. **RECALL PROCEDURES**

    1. *Health Hazard Evaluation*

        a. *An evaluation of the product being considered for recall will be conducted by plant management by examining:*

            i. *The nature of the defect.*
            ii. *Whether any illness or injuries have occurred from use of the product.*
            iii. *Assessment of the likelihood of occurrence of the hazard.*
            iv. *Assessment of potential consequences of occurrence of the hazard.*

    2. *Recall Classification will be assigned based on the health hazard evaluation.*

C. **RECALL STRATEGY**

    1. *This strategy will assist in, not dictate, the conduct of a recall. Using the recall classification assigned, the strategy will list:*

        a. *The amount of product being recalled.*
        b. *The extent of information being made available to customers or the public (including notices to the public and customers).*

      c.   The action plan to be used for the removal and return, correction, or destruction of the product.

  2. *Elements of the strategy will include:*

      a. *Results of the health hazard evaluation.*
      b. *Total amount of product involved (based on production records).*
      d. *Total product distribution (based on invoices containing code dating information).*
      e. *Action planned by recall (destination of product, FDA notification, public announcement, etc.).*
      d. *An investigation will occur that determines the cause of the recall.*

  3. *The Recall Strategy is implemented under the supervision of the Food Safety Director.*

  4. *Termination of Recall*

      a. *A recall will be considered concluded when plant management is satisfied that the recall action is completed, proper disposition has been made of the product in violation and no further emergency action is needed.*
      b. *FDA will be notified of any termination of recall.*

D. *Mock Recalls*

  1. *Mock recalls will be performed twice yearly and documented on the Product Recall Form. Documentation will include the date, time started and finished, amount of product produced, and amount of product recovered.*
  2. *Specifically, each recall will involve one lot of one product that has been processed at our facility. Any product remaining in the shipping freezer along with all customers who have received that product will be identified (based on physical verification and invoices including code dating information) and documented until all pieces or pounds of that product have been accounted for.*

Summary

Food safety is paramount for food processors today. Without it, unsafe food reaches consumers and Illness and death can result. When this happens, millions of dollars are spent, company reputations are ruined, and people's lives are destroyed.

This book focuses on food safety for food processors. First, it explores rules and regulations imposed by government agencies, customers, and the processing plants themselves (including GMP, SSOP, HACCP, Food Security, and Pest Control programs). Next, it analyzes the allergens and allergen programs used by food manufacturers. Last, but certainly not least, it examines the types of recalls and recall programs implemented by food processors when unsafe product reaches the public.

Congratulations! You now understand more about food safety...a critical aspect of food processing.

www.ingramcontent.com/pod-product-compliance
Lightning Source LLC
Chambersburg PA
CBHW070419190526
45169CB00003B/1325